Praise, Worship, and Thanksgiving

Praise, Worship, and Thanksgiving

Giving God What He Deserves

Audrey C. A. Eccleston

iUniverse, Inc.
Bloomington

Praise, Worship, and Thanksgiving
Giving God What He Deserves

iUniverse books may be ordered through booksellers or by contacting:

iUniverse
1663 Liberty Drive
Bloomington, IN 47403
www.iuniverse.com
1-800-Authors (1-800-288-4677)

ISBN: 978-1-4759-7080-7 (sc)
ISBN: 978-1-4759-7084-5 (ebk)

Printed in the United States of America

iUniverse rev. date: 04/17/2013

Dedication

I dedicate this book to my much beloved mother, Mrs Mable Muir, my family and all at the Church of God World Wide Mission (International) who I was honoured to leave when I joined my husband, the late Rev Basil Keith Eccleston at the Assemblies of the First Born Church (Harlesden). I owe a great debt in gratitude to both these congregations for their prayers and support. They have been a great source of strength and inspiration to me throughout my ministerial life.

ACKNOWLEDGEMENTS

Above all, I would like to give thanks and praise to Almighty God for his love and guidance throughout my life. I am indeed blessed with much spiritual blessings.

I also acknowledge the Principal, Rev T. Whyne, and all the staff at The Word of Life Theological College for their dedication and hard work that is evident in all of the lectures that are delivered. It was at the start of the course, that I was invited to join those leading a Time of Praise & Worship and this reinforced my passion for the theme Praise, Worship and Thanksgiving, which I later developed into a book.

In 2009, I was asked to be the Praise & Worship Co-ordinator for the AFB Convention held in London, Battersea. In 2010, I was asked to be the Administrator for the School of Worship at the New Testament Church of God (Brixton) and in 2011, I was asked to present a 3 hour Seminar to the Women's Convention at AFB (Derby) on Praise, Worship and Thanksgiving, by the President, Evangelist Margaret Seaton. Finally in 2012, I was able to complete my dissertation on this very topic, despite the passing of my dear husband. I have a reason to give God the Glory.

Contents

Introduction xi

PART 1: THEORY AND PRACTICE OF PRAISE 1

- a) Definition of Praise 1
  - i) The fruit of our lips 2
  - ii) A Sacrifice 2
  - iii) The Hebrew Meaning of Praise 3
- b) The Role of Praise and Worship Leaders (P&W Leaders) 4
- c) Why praise God? 8
- d) Acts of Praising God 10
- e) True Praises 11
- f) Some evidence from Scripture of results from praising God 11
- g) Who/What Praises God? 13
- h) Praise Songs 14
- i) The Power of Praise 15
- j) Unacceptable Praise: Attitudes when praising God 15

PART 2: THEORY AND PRACTICE OF WORSHIP 17

a) Definition of Worship: Why worship God? 17
b) Ignorant Worship, Vain Worship, True Worship........19
c) Acts of Worship..22
d) Worship Songs..28

PART 3: THE DIFFERENCE IN PRAISE AND WORSHIP 29

PART 4: THEORY AND PRACTICE OF THANKSGIVING 33

a) What is thanksgiving? 33
b) Why give thanks? 34
c) Thanksgiving Songs...35
d) How to praise, worship and thank God: In the spirit...35
e) Biblical evidence from praising God: Images 36
f) When faith is coupled with praise.............................40
g) Lessons from the evidence 41

Conclusion..43

Bibliography...45

INTRODUCTION

Praise, Worship and Thanksgiving is indicative of the state of a heart that is full of gratitude to God. All three words, collectively or individually makes one feel like uttering good things about God because one is satisfied with what God has done for them; releasing unspeakable joy. The English dictionary defines praise as a noun as: 'approval of merit; commendation';[1]in other words 'to admire; to glorify'. The Reader's Digest Reverse Dictionary states the definition of praise as a verb as: 'to recommend highly or talk about in an extremely enthusiastic way; to honour'.[2] The new Collins Thesaurus states that to praise is 'to magnify, to worship . . . to give thanks'.[3] I agree with all three of these definitions of praise and could not express it more succinctly. The meanings all resonate well. However, the Bible declares 'O give thanks unto the LORD; for he is good: for his mercy endureth for ever' (**Psalms 136:1**). King David not only gave thanks to God, he gave his reasons to be thankful. One of David's reasons was

---

1 Collins Double Book Enclyclopedia & Dictionary, Collins Clear Type Press, 1972, p 379

2 Reader's Digest Reverse Dictionary, 1st Edition, The Reader's Digest Association Limited, 1989, p 394

3 The New Collins Thesaurus, Guild Publishing London, 1985, p 516

that God was good and forever merciful to him. When David recognised the extent of God's goodness, he blurted out: 'I will bless the Lord at all times; his praise shall continually be in my mouth' (**Psalm 34: 1**). Can you see how the first three words of this paragraph are very much interconnected? Praise drives you to worship and having been worshipping God for a while, you naturally want to give thanks for the spiritual experience you had during the process. Could the three English dictionary definitions sighted above allow us to comprehend this all important topic: Praise, Worship and Thanksgiving? My research aims to reveal some of the power enveloped in it.

My research methodology will consist of qualitative evidence, some of which will be historical but authentic; and some of it will be experiential and inspirational. Having said that, if no primary source is found, numerous secondary sources documented in the Bible, other books and the Internet will be highlighted and scrutinised using arguments for and against to obtain a full understanding of Praise, Worship and Thanksgiving. I will explore this topic and examine why more and more people all over the world are so interested in rendering personal praise, corporate worship and thanksgiving to God, every time they get a chance to do so.

Since the Old Testament times many people have been compelled to give God the glory and be dependent on him for their good success. If you are not so inclined, I trust that after reading this study you too will realise the protection and source of strength that can be obtained through praising, worshipping and giving God thanks on a regular basis. The examples will speak for themselves and expose the tremendous power that a simple practice can achieve. You yourself will be challenged on several occasions 'to praise the Lord for his goodness' (**Psalm 107:8**).

✣

PART 1

THEORY AND PRACTICE OF PRAISE

a) Definition of Praise

'Praise' is what we offer to God for who He is/what He does despite how we feel, because our feelings change from time to time. King David of Israel declares in **Psalm 18:3** 'I will call upon the Lord who is worthy to be praised, so shall I be saved from mine enemies'. Here, David recognised that when he called upon God and uttered his praises, he felt safe and knew that his enemies could not hurt him. However, if we consider **Psalms 23:1** we observe how David relied on the Lord as his Shepherd. He described how God provided for him so that he lacked nothing. He remembered a time in his life when he was thirsty and the Lord gave him cool, still-water, as recorded in verse 2. Later in the Psalms, David realised he had divine protection from God, so he praised the Lord for shelter, safety and comfort. Right now, I am experiencing a new life in Jesus, ever since the day I asked Him to be my Saviour, in February 1972. Consequently, I join with one songwriter and say 'every time I get a chance to praise him, I will'.[4] However, far more is made of the concept of praise in the Old Testament than in the New Testament, especially in the Psalms, but it was Jesus who pointed out that babes and sucklings were the ones used to perfect praise in **Matthew 21:15-16.** The loudness of praising God is not just featured with the instruments used to praise him, but was recognised on 'the Mount of Olives when the whole multitude of the disciples began to rejoice and praise God with a loud voice for all the mighty works that they had done' (**Luke 19: 37**). Here we see God as Shepherd, Comforter and Saviour; for this we praise him.

i) The fruit of our lips

We give God the **highest praise** for He deserves it. "**Hallelujah!**" Paul exalts us to offer the sacrifice of praise as the fruit of our lips giving thanks to his name in **Hebrews 13:15.** Also, David encourages us to 'sing unto the Lord a new song; for he hath done marvellous things; his right hand and his holy arm, hath gotten him the victory' (**Psalms 98:1**). When we think of God's goodness we automatically admire and glorify the Lord, using expressed thoughts often conveyed in speech or song, so called the fruit of our lips.

ii) A Sacrifice

The new Collins Thesaurus defines ***sacrifice*** as a loss, something we forfeit, offer or give up. Therefore we understand that anything that costs someone dearly is a sacrifice. Paul again encourages

[4] Zie'l—Every time I get a chance to praise him - U-Tube

us to sacrifice our praise according to **Hebrews 13:15**, '. . . let us offer the sacrifice of praise to God continually'. What do you think about that? Admittedly, it's worth it.

What is your praise costing you?

Abraham offered a sacrificial praise offering to God when he obediently went to offer his only son, Isaac. Although the word "Praise" is mentioned 351 times in the Bible the English language has only one word for praise but in the original language there are 7 Hebrew words, each giving a different definition for praise.

iii) The Hebrew Meaning of Praise

HEBREW—ENGLISH TRANSLATION[5]

1. **Shabach**—To shout praise specifically in a loud tone (**Daniel 2:23; 4:37**)

2. **Tehillah**—To sing praise; Song of praise; Hymn praise (**Psalms 111:1**)

3. **Halal**—To boast God's goodness; to show forth his praises (**Jeremiah 51:41**)

4. **Yadah**—To throw out the hands upwards asking God to help us or lift us up, to bemoan by wringing the hands

[5] AMG'S Annotated Strong's Hebrew Dictionary of the Old Testament, 2003, AMG Publishers, ISBN 978-0-89957-746-3.

whilst worshipping God; to worship with extended hands. **(Psalms 63:4; Nehemiah 8:6)**

5. **Barak**—To declare God as the source of everything, to bless and thank God, to bend the knee in blessing.

6. **Todah**—To praise and thank God together

7. **Zamar**—To praise with a stringed instrument plucking the tune of a song

b) The Role of Praise and Worship Leaders (P&W Leaders)

'Christian Worship is often thought of as the music portion of a church service where people sing songs to God.'[6] I strongly disagree with this statement because I have reason to believe Christian Worship is far more than this. However, I agree with this statement, in part, for music aids worship. Analytically, if we only consider the English word ***worship,*** we understand that it comes from two Old English words: "weorth"[7] meaning ***worth*** and "scripe" or "ship" which means ***shape or quality***, according to Andy Pittman. This same Old English word "ship" is used, as the suffix in words like sportsmanship in modern words to express the quality of being a good sport. Thus the quality of having worth or being worthy can be derived from ***weorth-ship***

[6] http://ask.com What is Christian Worship?

[7] http://blogspot.co.uk 40 days of Prayer: Worship, Sunday, March 12, 2011.

which means to ascribe greatness to God and so we declare God worthy of praise when we worship him, by engaging our hearts, voices and hands stretched towards Heaven. Those who have the responsibility of leading Praise and Worship should exercise their right, according to **Proverbs 6:27** for 'as a man thinketh . . . so is he'. They should be armed with the Word of God in their hearts and minds when they stand to lead. Much preparation is needed for this role. Prayer and fasting is necessary and a willingness to be directed by the Holy Spirit is vital for that servant of God. There is no doubt that the leader must first be properly prepared, having surrendered his/her life to Jesus Christ to deal with issues that may arise in the process. Therefore, singing spiritual songs is simply not enough. Why is it important to understand this?

It is not only important but essential. Primarily, the job of such an individual is to bring the congregation into the presence of God publicly and reverently, by whatever way he/she sees it fit at the time. How is this done? Sometimes, a few words of encouragement are given; sometimes a quote from Scripture, with the correct emphasis, is appropriate and sometimes all one has to do is to shout **Hallelujah! Praise the Lord!** At other times, the leader may just state **Psalms 95: 6**, 'O Come, let us worship and bow down, let us kneel before the Lord our maker'. Here, for instance, a simple request made from Scripture invites the congregation to come together and have the same mind to worship at that time. Some people in the congregation who are spiritually alert will respond immediately because they understand the move of God; others follow the leading of the Holy Spirit.

During the worship activity, it is the **P&W** Leader who would not hesitate to raise the standard of worship. Instinctively, that is why part of the role of the worship leader is being able to recognise this and bring the congregation to acknowledge the presence of God, for God is moving by his Spirit. The Bible tells us 'God is a spirit and they that worship him must worship him in the spirit and in truth' in **Philippians 3:3** but, 'what is the meaning of Christian Worship?'[8] Many people know that the Holy Spirit has to reside in the hearts of those who worship God, since it makes sense to have such a connection. If you do not know the awesome facts (that which is called truth) about God how can you adore him? You would not be able to start to describe and declare his might and power; for it is when we remind God of his greatness, among other attributes, that we worship him. How we worship him might take various forms, such as Art and Drama depending on how creative we want to be in our worship. This is why I endorse the statement: 'All worship is a response to truth, and that which is truth is contained in the Word of God,'[9] quoted in the article: What is the meaning of Christian Worship?

As P&W Leaders, we must seek God's help for what to do and say in each service, particularly special Services like Missionary and Evangelistic, where people come with various needs expecting miracles. In times like these, the power of our praise enables us to break into the supernatural realm where miracles happen. We must be anointed vessels of honour in our daily walk and allow

[8] http://www.gotquestions.org/Christian—worship.html/
What is the meaning of Christian Worship?

[9] http://www.gotquestions.org/Christian—worship.html.

the Spirit to move amongst us. We must be mature in God and able to set the platform/stage for the Preacher to preach. We must be appointed by God to pull down the walls of Basham and/or remove the spirit of heaviness, when necessary, during the service. Why? This is because we are responsible for the atmosphere of miracles during the service. Nowadays, we mainly operate at 3 points during a service, singing with understanding:

i) at the start of the service to drive the clouds away/dispel any unfamiliar spirit lurking around

ii) when the offering is being collected or when we worship God in our cheerful giving

iii) and during the Altar Call when we sow spiritual seeds linking the preached Word with the words we used to minister the refrain/chorus being sung.

The term ***worship leader*** 'really didn't emerge until the early 1970s'[10]. Apart from singing hymns, most churches sing Scripture choruses but now they are overwhelmed by worship music and worship leaders leading Christ-exalting songs during the service; and not just song leaders and choral directors as usual. Nowadays, many Christians see themselves as worshippers in the House of God. What a change in attitude and behaviour in the 21 Century! There is liberty where the presence of the Lord is.

---

[10] Webber, Robert, E. 1996, Blended Worship: Achieving Substance and Relevance in Worship (Hendrickson Publishers, IBSN 1-56563245-1) p51

I join with Bob Kauflin when he states that we, as P&W leaders, should not 'wonder if we're doing something wrong' . . . 'and start to think we'd be more effective if we looked, sounded and acted like the worship-leaders everyone knows'[11]. No! Let us be faithful and not be tempted to copy what we see and hear around us for God accepts our worship offering too; ancient and modern. However, here is a word of caution for P&-Worship-leaders: We must remember 'the call to be faithful'[12] to God and not seek to become famous, because marketing church music, and DVDs has become successful; likewise have the popular worship artists, their concert tours and interviews. Evidently, it is possible not to be tempted by fame. 'Matt Redman is one of many internationally known worship leaders who think of himself not as a star but a humble servant.[13]

c) Why praise God?

We have our own reasons for praising God depending on what God did for us. King David stated 'For from birth I have relied on you' **(Psalms 71:6).** What are YOU saying to God today?

* **Because of what God has done: this will change your situation for good**

[11] Bob Kauflin, Worship Matters, Leading others to encounter the greatness of God, p57

[12] Bob Kauflin, 2008, Worship Matters p57

[13] Bob Kauflin, 2008 Worship Matters, p58

Some people praise God while they are going through certain situations and the power in their praise allow them to get the victory. Their circumstances change somehow. For instance, when Paul and Silas of the Bible were imprisoned because of the Gospel, they sang and praised God throughout their ordeal and at midnight something miraculous happened according to **Acts 16:25**. The record revealed that suddenly a great earthquake that shook the foundations of the prison and immediately, not only were all the doors of the prison opened but everyone's bands were loosed. From what happened on this occasion, we see how the power of praise got Paul and Silas their victory. When they were arrested they realised that the gift of salvation, which they received from Jesus was a powerful tool from God so they rejoiced in their salvation and praised God, since they had experienced the joy of knowing Jesus Christ. It was whilst they were giving God the glory that their miracle happened at that prison, in Jerusalem. Being aware of what God had done in the past allows us to praise him during insurmountable crisis and through faith experience a change for the better. Paul and Silas' time of praise and worship was a declaration of the Gospel to those in the prison; this being the last thing on their minds.

- **For He hath delivered me from mine enemies.**

In the book of **2 Samuel 22:1-4**, David focuses on thanksgiving for God's powerful deliverance. David stated 'I will call upon the Lord who is worthy to be praised, so shall I be saved from mine enemies'. That day when the Lord delivered him out of the hand of Saul, David penned these words and made it into a song. Why? Because He realised that his God was alive for he saved him from violence, in verse 4. **What are YOUR reasons to praise God today?** Dear reader you might like to reflect on your own life for a moment. Do not be afraid to praise God because you are being led by the Spirit of God and may not know it.

d) Acts of Praising God

We can use the words of refrains, songs, Scripture, prayers and poems to praise God. According to **Psalms 34:1-4,** David said 'I will bless the Lord at all times; His praise shall continually be in my mouth'.

In **Nehemiah 8:6** we see how Ezra blessed the Lord, the great God. 'And all the people answered Amen, Amen with lifting up their hands and they bowed their heads and worshipped the Lord with their faces to the ground'. Notice here that everyone gave reverence to God together (at the same time). Notice here also, that as well as using their hands, heads and voices, in this case, the people were united in their actions. Also, in **2 Chronicles 5:12-14,** we read how one environment was transformed spiritually when the people praised the Lord; saying 'For he is good; for his mercy endureth for ever'; that then the house was filled with a cloud, even the house of the Lord'. We are told that in that moment, not even the priests could stand to minister by reason of the cloud: for the glory of the Lord had filled the house of God. This is another way we can get God's attention, simply by talking about his goodness and his everlasting mercy towards his people. His presence filled the atmosphere round about us in times like these, when we gather and remind him of his faithfulness.

e) True Praises

One songwriter said:

I offer up to you praises from my heart
That they may be in truth
A perfect sacrifice
To show my gratitude
For all the things you do
I just want to give true praises from my heart
Lord I give to you true praises from my heart

(Mark Beswick)

True praise can only come from a heart that is honest to God. Here the writer gave his reason as wanting to show gratitude for the things God did in his life.

David reminds us in **Psalms 29:2 to:** 'Give unto the Lord the Glory due unto His Name, worship the Lord in the beauty of holiness'. We can praise God for what we know about Him. For example declare his attributes: He is Loving, Kind, Merciful, Just, Holy, Righteous, Omnipotent, Faithful, Invisible, Omnipresent . . .

f) Some evidence from Scripture of results from praising God

<u>The glory of the Lord will come down:</u>

At the inauguration of the Temple in the days of King Solomon, the cloud which descended upon those present was the symbol of God's glory and it filled the house, which was being dedicated for the first time in the house of God. Notice here that it was while the people were saying the same thing that God made his presence felt (**2 Chronicles 5:2-6; 10-14**). In verse 13, it is clear that they were all united—'as the trumpeters and singers were **as one**, to make **one sound** to be praising and thanking the Lord; and when they lifted up their voice with the trumpets and cymbals and instruments of music and praised the Lord; that then the house was filled with a cloud, even the house of the Lord.' What can we learn from this? Observe here that the people came before the Lord with singing and as they began to praise and magnify the Lord, God began to take His rightful place in their midst. Could we learn from this how to access God's presence? I can see why one songwriter wrote the words:

> *Jesus we enthrone you, we proclaim you our King . . .*
> *We raise you up with our praise . . .*
> *Come Lord Jesus and take your place.*
>
> ***(Don Moen)***

Perhaps, the songwriter could visualise Jesus as the King of kings standing in the middle of the congregation while they were worshipping. On reflection he could see Jesus taking his rightful position and even encouraged him to do so, in the last clause. When we 'sing songs that say something'[14] 'public worship functions in a purely educative manner'[15] and the words we sing

[14] Bob Kauflin, Worship Matters, Leading others to encounter the greatness of God, 2008, p101

[15] Pater Noster, Creation at Worship, Ecology, Creative and Christian Worship, 1995, p43

are received and remembered well by those hearing them for the very first time. So we are proclaiming and involving the person that is not yet a Christian believer by our worship; contrary to the question Christopher J. Voke asked: 'Worship—proclaiming or involving?'[16]

TASK: Hands up if you ever had an experience like that. This will happen only at the point when we are all on ONE ACCORD in the service i.e. musicians, singers, leaders and congregation whether clapping or shouting, but praising God in unison. It is us that will make the connection happen when we are in tune with the Holy Spirit, in that moment in time; as in the Upper Room experience according to **Acts 2: 1-4.**

g) Who/What Praises God?

Angels, the Saints, the Creation and Nature praise God

According to New Testament, angels spend all their time praising him with the words: 'Holy, holy, holy, Lord God Almighty, which was and is and is to come . . . Thou art worthy, O Lord to receive glory and honour and power; for thou hast created all things, and for thy pleasure they are and were created'. (**Rev 4:8, 11; Psalms 148:2**)

In the Book of Psalms, believers praise the Lord with a new song and dance (**Psalms 149**). 'Kings of the Earth and all people, princes

[16] Pater Noster, Creation at Worship, p43

and all judges of the Earth . . . for his name alone is excellent.' There is a unique aspect of praise highlighted in this Psalm by the saints of God, whom God will use to establish his kingdom on the Earth. All creation in particular, the sun, moon and stars in the heavens praise God (**Psalms 148**); and in **Psalms 150** even the instruments of music is included 'in everything' because we use them to praise the Lord. Here we see that the sound of the trumpet, psaltery and harp . . . and stringed instruments and organs were used to praise the Lord from Old Testament times. We are reminded in **Psalms 96:11-12**, how 'the heavens rejoice', 'the Earth be glad', 'the sea roar', 'the field be joyful' and 'the trees of the wood rejoice'. All creatures—Everything that hath breath—every man, woman and their children are exhorted to praise God (**Psalms 150:6**). Praise is a weapon in the believer's armoury. Do you know how to use this weapon? How many times have you used this weapon this year? Have you done so already today?

h) Praise Songs

1. *We are together again just praising the Lord*

2. *We praise your name O Lord*

3. *Hallelujah! Praise the Lamb*

4. *Glory and honour and praises*

5. *Let's just praise the Lord, praise the Lord*

i) The Power of Praise

When the Ammorites, Moabites and the children of Mount Seir came against Judah, King Jehoshaphat and the children of Judah sought the Lord for help. With the assurance that 'the battle was not yours, but God's' (verse 15); they sent their army led by the Praise Team against their enemies. (**2 Chronicles 20: 22-31**) What was the result when they followed the instructions given?

The result of this event in the history of Judah illustrates that there is Power in Praise to God, so let us be obedient and follow God's instructions having faith in Him. In the light of this, do we need to follow instructions given by our leaders? Oh yes, we should 'trust and obey for there is no other way to be happy in Jesus, but to trust and obey'[17].

j) Unacceptable Praise: Attitudes when praising God

Jesus reminds us that Isaiah the prophet spoke about people who pretend to praise God with their lips only. According to **Matthew 15:7-9** we understand that Jesus noticed that the people drew nigh to God with their mouths and honoured him with their lips but their hearts were far from him. Is our sacrifice of praise accepted by God? When Abraham prepared his sacrifice and placed it on the altar it was accepted when at sunset he noticed a flame passed through it signifying that God was pleased with it (**Genesis 15: 9, 10, 17**).

[17] Redemption Songs, 1000 Hymns and Choruses, Hymn 459, HarperCollins Publishers, ISBN 0007212372

If we regard iniquity in our hearts the Lord will not hear us. We must have a free course to access God's throne room at any moment, so that our praise can be accepted. As we approach God our hearts must be humble and respectful so that God would draw near to us. Scripture tells us to 'Be careful for nothing but with prayer and supplication and don't forget thanksgiving, make your request unto the Lord' (**Philippians 4:6**) because our attitudes must be right before we can begin to praise God.

Attitudes when praising God include being:

1. Truthful (**St John 4:23**)
2. Spiritual (**Philippians 3:3**)
3. Full of Praise (**Psalms 51:15-19**)
4. Peaceful (**Amos 5:22-24**)
5. Joyful (**1 Chronicles 15:16**)
6. Thankful (**Psalms 118:1**)

PART 2

THEORY AND PRACTICE OF WORSHIP

a) Definition of Worship: Why worship God?

'Worship is an active response to God whereby we declare His worth. Worship is not passive, but is participative. Worship is not simply a mood; it is a response. Worship is not just a feeling; it is a declaration'.[18] Like Allen and Borror, I strongly believe that worship is a declaration. I subscribe to the notion that mankind was born with the capacity to adore something; this ability to adore someone or something is what is referred to as worship. Some people worship artwork, pets, other people, cars, idols, music whilst others worship the True and Living God. They spend a lot of time with the love of their life. They think about it, they talk about it and dream about it because they so love it. It is clear

[18] Ronald Allen and Gordon Borror, 1982, Re-discover the Missing Level or Multnomah, p16.

that one cannot worship something until they love it very much (**Joshua 24:14**).

On the contrary, most people do not worship God. They miss out big—time on a great experience. I know that worship is a way to embrace the presence of God and I feel honoured when I can. Some people skip about, others dance and many walk around and shout praises in that moment, because they feel good in God's presence. I agree with Bob Grass when he concludes that: 'when we fail to worship God we always find a substitute, even if it ends up being ourselves.'[19] 'Worship is the entire attitude of one's life or being in relationship to God the Creator,'[20] which takes on many forms culturally and historically according to Yoshiaki Hattori. Is this possible?

Evidently, several mega churches have sprung up in recent years, all over the world, and many of them seem to have mastered the act of rendering praise, corporate worship and thanksgiving to God publicly. On many occasions an atmosphere of miracles is created and many people derived spiritual benefit from just simply being present for the Worship Service. How comes? It is during this time that a divine connection is made, when everyone is tuned to the frequency of the Holy Spirit. At this point, all the glory is unto the Lord for only He is worthy of our praise and sentiments echo the words: You are awesome in this place Mighty God!

---

[19] http://www.Praise-and-worship.com Praise and worship the God of the Bible for he is holy and righteous

[20] Yoshiaki Hattari, (1982), Worship: Adoration and Action, Theology of Worship in the Old Testament, Portland, p 21

b) Ignorant Worship, Vain Worship, True Worship

<u>What/who are we worshipping?</u>

In **Acts 17:23** Paul came across some people worshipping at an altar with the inscription TO THE UNKNOWN GOD. This is ignorant worship since the people did not know the name of the god they were worshipping; so Paul preached a sermon from Mars' hill entitled 'God will judge the world by Jesus Christ'. I can hear the message in a chorus:

Call Him by His name . . . Call Him by His name . . .

Call Him by His name . . . Call Him by His name . . .

JESUS . . . JESUS . . . JESUS . . . JESUS . . .

Since we already know that there is healing and deliverance in the Name of Jesus, we aught to proclaim Scriptural truths[21] as Bob Kauflin recommends we do. Also, in **1 Peter 2:9,** Peter tells us that we have been saved 'that we may proclaim the excellencies of him who called us out of darkness into his marvellous light' daily. For example, here we are saying that this name really matters, so we place great emphasis on it declaring it as something very important. This is why sometimes without warning the Praise-leader might sing a song/chorus to minister to the needs of someone, anonymous but present, in the congregation. We should

[21] Bob Kaflin, Worship Matters, Leading others to encounter the greatness of God, 2008, p 129

be sensitive to the leading of the Holy Spirit and flow with the Spirit; allowing the Spirit move and work at that moment. The Apostle John declares that God is a Spirit and they that worship him must worship him in Spirit and truth (**St John 4:24**). Let's not worship God ignorantly but mature in God and train younger believers to do likewise.

Matthew 15: 7-9 describes vain worship as when people who draw near to God with their mouth and honour him with their lips, but their hearts far from him. They were called hypocrites by Jesus (verse 7) because they taught the commandments of men as doctrines, so God used Isaiah to prophesy to them, according to the Gospel of Matthew.

This is worship that focuses on satisfying self but not praising God. An example of this is 'Audience centred worship' like the kind we see on TV sometimes. Let us be careful of this because such worship will never be pleasing to God. In **Amos 5: 21-23** we see what worship without righteousness results in. This kind of worship is despised by God and is not accepted and we are told that God says to 'take away from him the noise of our songs; for he will not hear the melody of our viols,' by his deliberate choice.

I can confirm what the next quote states: 'True worship is not about us, it's all about God . . . because it's about God's will for us and not the other way around.'[22] This idea is further reinforced by the Apostle John who points us to the true-worshippers in **St John**

[22] http://www.praise-and-worship.com

4: 23-24; 'But the hour is coming when the true worshippers will worship the Father in Spirit and truth; for the Father is seeking such to worship Him'. True worshippers will worship from their hearts, having no confidence in the flesh. They will circumcise their hearts and allow the spirit of God to dwell richly there. Worship then becomes a lifestyle, in keeping with what Martin Luther said: 'A dairymaid milk cows to the glory of God'. This suggests that if we do everything as unto the Lord, that is, we would be worshipping God 24/7.

Darlene Zschech wrote: 'We often hear the phrase "Worship is a lifestyle" but what does it really mean?'[23] In my opinion, this singer/songwriter/worshipper has asked a very pertinent question that sits at the heart of where we are when we worship God. We cannot worship with sin in our hearts for God will not accept our worship. His love will melt our hearts when we approach him in spirit and in truth. It is said that tears are a language that God understands and realise that we have to live with clean hands, a pure heart and a right spirit for God to dwell within us. In other words, the statement means we have to be godly at all times; doing the right thing; that is, while we go about our daily work, at school, at play and not just when we meet at our place of worship. Why? Almighty God knows us through and through and will not accept anything less than holiness and righteousness from us. He is faithful and just and loves to reach down to us when we are honest and cry to him. I hope that it is more obvious now than ever that worship is not all about songs but about our relationship with our Creator.

[23] http://www.higherpraise.com/worship/worship_worshipisalifestyle

c) Acts of Worship

When we use our various body parts to express what we feel, this is indicative of how we respond to God's transforming power; demonstrating that our worship is alive. 'We have been touched and we've responded to God's transforming power'[24] as we enter the glory of his presence.

<u>**The use of hands:**</u> - Beseeching, outstretched hands
- To wave your hands, to clap your hands
- To reach out to God, to lift your hands **(Psalms 134:2).**

One songwriter captured the moment in the following refrain:

I lift my hand in the sanctuary
I lift my hands to give you the glory
I lift my hands to give you the praise . . . days
(Kirk Franklin)

<u>**The use of the full range of our body movements: head, hands, feet and legs**</u>

* Bowing down (**Psalms 95:6); Psalms 149:3**)

It was King David of the Bible who invited us to 'worship and bow down' in one of his psalm of praise to the great God.

---

[24] Webber, Robert, E. (1996), Blended Worship, p97

* Clapping (**Psalms 47:1**)

Again King David urges us to clap our hands as part of our worship act in verse 1 of Psalm 47 but Isaiah noticed that even the trees clap their hands when there is joy (**Isaiah 55:12**). However, when Zion was under judgement, Jeremiah, the prophet saw that 'all that pass by clap their hands' at the children of Israel; 'they hiss and wag their head at the daughter of Jerusalem, saying, Is this the city that men call The perfection of beauty, The Joy of the whole earth?' (**Lamentation 2:15**) From this we observe that the clapping of hands is a key gesture that is used to draw attention to something or someone on certain instances.

* Lifting hands (**Psalms 63:4; 1 Timothy 2:8**)

David told the Lord that while he yet lived 'I will lift up my hands in thy name'. Raising his hands seemed like a kind of gesture made when he wanted God to reach down and lift him up; just what a small child would do when adults are around and he/she feels safe.

* Dancing (**2 Sam 6:14; Psalms 150:4**)

According to the Book of Samuel, King David 'danced before the Lord with all his might and David was girded with a linen ephod' and he later encouraged the saints to praise the Lord with a dance, in verse 4 of his final Psalm.

* Leaping . . . jumping up, springing up (**Acts 3:8; Acts 14:10; Luke 6:23**)

In the Book of Acts, Chapter 3, Verse 8, Peter took the man who was lame from his mother's womb by the hand and lifted him up and immediately his feet and ankle bone received strength . . . 'And he leaping up stood, and walked, and entered with them into the temple, walking, and leaping and praising God'. Another time, when Paul and Barnabas were preaching the Gospel in Lystra, there was a certain man, impotent in his feet, because he was a cripple from his mother's womb and had never walked. Paul commanded him with a loud voice to 'stand upright on thy feet' and the man leaped and walked, according to **Acts14:9-10** for he had faith to be healed. It is clear to see that leaping is that sudden rise to one's feet instantaneously—the moment faith is reached. In the Beatitudes, Jesus himself also admonished his followers to leap for joy, as their fathers did before the prophets of old when they were reproached for the Son of man's sake; knowing that their reward is great in heaven (**Luke 6;23**).

* Kneeling (**Psalms 95:6**); **Isaiah 45:23**)

David exhorts the saints (those who made a covenant with God) to 'come let us kneel before the Lord our maker' in **Psalm 95 verse 6**. However, Isaiah declared that Salvation will come only by the Lord when 'every knee shall bow' to the Saviour in **verse 23 of Isaiah 45**. Somehow to bend the knee or fall on the knee or to rest on the knee in prayer is indicative of submitting to a higher power than ourselves. When we kneel in deep contrition; it is in those moments that God sees our weakness and helps us through our difficulties. Hallelujah!

The use of my mouth, lips and whole heart

* Singing (**Psalms 63:5; Psalms 89:1; Hebrews: 13-15; Psalms 61:8; Psalms 59:16-17**).

In **Psalms 63:5**, David penned these words 'my mouth shall praise thee with joyful lips' when he realised that God satisfied his thirsty soul (**Psalms 63:5**). Sometimes Scripture is used for the words of the song, refrain or chorus as with **Psalm 89:1.**

1. *I will sing of the mercies of the Lord forever I will sing,*
   I will sing
   I will sing of the mercies of the Lord forever,
   I will sing of the mercies of the Lord

2. *Sing praises unto God sing praises; sing praises unto God sing praises. Alleluia* (**Psalms 47:6-7**)

David gave reasons why he praised God with his whole heart (**Psalms 111:1; Psalms 138:1**) when he declares that God keeps his covenants and perfects that which concerns him.

* Shouting (**Psalms 47:1**)

David encouraged us to 'shout unto God with the voice of triumph' and in **2 Samuel 6:15** David and all the house of Israel brought up the ark of the Lord with shouting and with the sound of the trumpet'. In **Joshua 6:10,** Joshua gave clear instructions regarding the moment when all the people should 'shout with a great shout' (verse 5). This was the moment the walls of Jericho fell flat so that the children of Israel gained the victory.

* Praying (**Revelation 5:8; Psalms 61:1**)

We are reminded by John the Revelator that the prayers of the saints are kept in golden vials full of odours, but King David never ceased to praise God according to the Book of Psalm; 'Evening, and morning, and at noon will I pray and cry aloud: and he shall hear my voice' **Psalms 55:17**. Here we see that David prayed morning, noon and night to his Creator. We also see in **Daniel 6:11** that the mischievous men in Babylon assembled and found Daniel praying and making supplication before his God during King Darius' reign.

* Speaking to yourselves in psalms, hymns and spiritual songs (**Ephesians 5:19-20**); and in tongues (**1 Corinthians 14:2**).

The Apostle Paul exhorts us to speak to ourselves in this manner for this enables us to be grateful to God for what he has done for us. Later Paul tells us that when we speak in an unknown tongue, we speak not unto man but unto God. He also explains that tongues are used 'for a sign not to them that believe, but to them that believe not' (**1 Corinthians 14:22**).

* Songs (**Psalms 69:30**)

Like David, many of us pledge 'to praise the name of God with a song and magnify him with thanksgiving'; why? This is simply because we recognise the blessing of Almighty God on our lives so we are being careful for nothing therefore show gratitude.

<u>**The use of the full range of our voices:**</u>

* In singing, shouting, praying, preaching, teaching, reading and declaring Scripture we always express our feelings to God, depending on where we are, but it is all included in the term ***worship***.

<u>**The use of musical instruments: (Psalms 149:3), Psalms 150:3-6), (11 Chronicles 5:12)**</u>

* Key-boards, timbrels, tambourines, organs, guitars, drums, harps, trumpet, lire, lutes, strings and pipes, clashing cymbals, cornets and the human voice

The role of music is to aid the efforts of our praising voices, so let us remember that we are working towards giving God the best praise. I agree with Robert Webber's statement: 'Worshipping churches are discovering the freeing experiences of using the body in worship'[25] because we see this in live-worship, at Gospel Concerts and on DVD's over the last decade, worldwide.

d) Worship Songs

1. No other name but the name of Jesus

[25] Webber, R. E. 1996, Blended Worship, p171

2. Hallelujah, Hallelujah for the Lord God Almighty Reigns
3. Glory and honour and praises, glory and honour to Jesus
4. I worship you Almighty God, there is none like You
5. Bow down and worship him
6. Holy Spirit rain down
7. How great thou art
8. You deserve the glory and the honour

PART 3

THE DIFFERENCE IN PRAISE AND WORSHIP

God is God and He is always worthy to be praised no matter what our circumstances because of all the marvellous things He has already done for us. Praise usually precedes worship and often ushers us into worship mode. **Praise** is a person's positive reaction to what God has done for them or who He is recognised to be in his/her life. Therefore, we use our lips, hearts and souls to convey our appreciation of God's love for us. Praise is not praise until it is heard because how would you know if someone wanted to praise you until they spoke something good into your ears. **Worship** is our reaction to a revelation of what God has done or of who God is. It causes us to also use our hands (in gesture to ask for things) and our heads and bodies (to bow down before Him) while we engage in honouring Him. This is certainly more dramatic in expression than just standing up or sitting down talking or singing to God. Worshipping him is more energetic than praising him; our intensity is greater.

What might we expect to happen during Praise?

1. The Glory of YHWH descended in the place where the people assembled themselves before the ark, as in the days of King Solomon in the new temple. (**2 Chronicles 5: 2-6; 11-14**)

2. The victory brought forward when Jehoshaphat received the Word which came from God. He demonstrated FAITH in God when he sent singers to the Front Line to give praise to God for what He had already promised to do and secured the victory (**2 Chronicles 20: 1-30**).

3. The release of Paul and Silas from a prison cell in Philippi (**Acts 16:26**).

Could this happen at the place where you worship God?

Oh yes. It is only when we respond to God's anointed Word in our own lives that we will experience and know the victory that He has promised. When we draw close to God through praises, He comes and inhabits the praises and we are released from things which bound us e.g. sin, evil spirits, prison, sickness and diseases . . . or any situation of hardship. The believer is liberated and is freed from spiritual bondage by the powerful presence of God. This is what is referred to as the anointing that breaks the yoke on us. Have you not heard testimonies of people who have had experience like this? With 21st Century Technology we can now witness yokes being broken, from the comfort of our homes.

Also, anointed musicians, like David, can just play a tune and a transformation from spiritual bondage takes place. In many churches today we have musical renditions, some of which touch our souls, make us cry and stand on our feet to worship God spontaneously. Many become aware of this moment and recognise the presence of God as he inhabits our musical-praise, by standing with outstretched arms as we glorify his name. It is only a pity that not everyone present has the same understanding of what is happening—God is accepting our praise-offering. This is why those who have spiritual insight should lead by example so that the whole congregation will be blessed.

Evidence from Scripture

- When the evil spirit from God was upon Saul, David took the harp and played with his hand; so Saul was refreshed, and was well and the evil spirit departed from him (**1 Samuel 16:23**).

- When the kings of Israel, Judah and Edom thought they had lost the battle in the wilderness; Elisha the Prophet called for a minstrel to play and the power of YHWH came upon him and he prophesied that there would be water for everyone in Israel, Judah and Edom and that Lord would deliver the Moabites into their hands (**2 Kings 3:17**).

Notice here that there were no lyrics. The musicians expressed their praise in musical form, bringing the anointing of God upon the congregation to dispel those things that are troubling them: SKILFUL, SERIOUS PLAYING.

PART 4

THEORY AND PRACTICE OF THANKSGIVING

a) What is thanksgiving?

Thanksgiving is an expression of gratitude especially to God.

* For centuries ancient civilisations held ***harvest thanksgiving*** celebrations: 'In Britain we have given thanks for Harvest Thanksgiving since pagan times.'[26]

* 'Thanksgiving is celebrated annually by the Americans and the Canadians since 1621 when the English Pilgrims shared it with the natives who taught them how to survive the harsh winters of the New World.'[27] We thank God for the rain, the sunshine, food, shelter, health and strength, peace of mind, friends and so much more.

---

[26] http://enwikipedia.org/wiki/Harvest Festivals
[27] http://en.wikipedia.org

- * In the book of Philippians we are reminded that we should **NEVER FORGET TO SAY THANKS.** Paul tells us to 'be careful for nothing, but with prayer and supplication and don't forget thanksgiving let your request known to the Lord'.

  (Philippians 4:6).

b) Why give thanks?

King David, a man after God's owns heart reminds us:

- It is a good thing to give thanks unto the Lord . . . (**Psalms 92:1-2**) for faithful that promised.

Go ahead and think about God's love, his goodness and where he has brought you from. Don Moen invites us to do just that in the words of his song, ***"Think about his love"*** so be encouraged and think about what God has done for YOU personally to date and then GIVE Him THANKS and PRAISE for all you can remember. Now reflect on this brief experience and see how good it makes you feel.

c) Thanksgiving Songs

1. All good gifts around us are sent from heaven above, so thank the Lord

2. Many are the blessings that you give unto me

3. Thank you Lord, thank you Lord

4. Oh Give Thanks, unto the Lord for He is good

d) How to praise, worship and thank God: In the spirit

According to **St John 4: 23-24,** Jesus told the Samaritan woman that 'the hour cometh, and now is, when the true worshipper shall worship the father in spirit and in truth: for the Father seeketh such to worship him. GOD IS A SPIRIT and they that worship him must worship him in spirit and in truth'. When she realised this fact, she left her water pot, ran into the city and told the men that she has seen Christ, the Messiah—The Anointed One. The spirit in this woman made her start evangelising the city straight away with the truth she had found out. I am sure her heart was full of gratitude as she was spreading the good news. She could speak easily about what she had found and joyfully conveyed it to all those she came into contact with. Is not this the great commission given by our Lord Jesus Christ? (**Mathew 28:19-20**) Let us go into the world and let people know about Jesus and his works. Through the Holy Spirit, God will perform a work in those who believe, because 'it is not by might it is not by power but by my spirit, saith the Lord.' This Samaritan woman really did know how to praise, worship and thank God for her blessings. She did it with joy and gladness in her heart and was willing to confess everything about herself, so that the light of God could shine through her and dispel all manner of darkness in her life. There was a right spirit within her causing her to respond to God's love and mercy.

e) Biblical evidence from praising God: Images

1. When Joshua fought the Battle of Jericho he was given specific instructions which were followed by everyone and the walls came tumbling down (**Joshua 6:20**). It started when Joshua looked up and beheld the captain of the host of the Lord came to him (verse 13-14) with his sword drawn in his hand. Joshua worshipped God and enquired if the Lord sent any message to his servant. Joshua was told to loose his shoes from off his feet for the place where he stood was holy. Then the Lord revealed to Joshua that he had given Jericho, that great city. All he had to do was to be obedient to the letter. He and his soldiers were to:

   - go around the city once a day for six days (verse 3)

   - and seven priests were to bear before the ark seven trumpets of rams' horn, as they passed before the Lord

   - and on the 7th day they should go around the city seven times

   - and blow with the trumpets

     - and when they made **a long blast** and heard the sound of the trumpet, all the people should shout with a great shout at that time (verse 10).

'So the walls of the city fell down and Joshua's fame was noised throughout all the country' because they witnessed what God had done through Joshua's childlike obedience in the war situation. Oh that all men would obey God when he speaks to us, for we would see the glory of God and learn to trust him more.

2. When the Levites gave praise and thanks to the Lord then the temple was filled with a cloud signifying the presence of the Lord. (**2 Chronicles 5:13-14**) It was the moment 'the trumpeters and singers **were as one,** to make one sound to be heard in praising and thanking the Lord; and when they lifted

up their voice with the trumpets and cymbals and instruments of musick, and praised the Lord, For *he is* good and his mercies *endureth* for ever: that then the house was filled with a cloud . . . for the glory of the Lord had filled the house of the Lord'.

3. When Daniel refused to conform to King Darius' degree, according to the law of the Medes and Persians, which change not, God preserved him. The law stated that 'whosoever shall ask a petition of any God or man for thirty days; save of thee, O king, he shall be cast into the den of lions'. Daniel continued to worship God in his heart. Daniel went into his house; and his windows being opened in his chamber toward Jerusalem, he kneeled upon his knees three times a day and prayed and gave thanks before his God, as did aforetime' (**Daniel 6:10**). When this news reached the king, he commanded that Daniel was cast into the den of lions. The king at the same time prophesied to Daniel because he added, 'Thy God whom thou servest continually, he will deliver thee' (**Daniel 6:16**). The result was that the lions that were sent to devour him in the den, they became his friends. Notice here, the alteration of the expected end, through the obedience and true worship of the Living God by Daniel, God's servant (**Daniel 6:22**). For the king went early the next morning unto the den of lions to check Daniel's fate. Daniel replied 'My God hath sent his angel, and hath shut the lions' mouths, that they have not hurt me: for as much as before him innocence was found in me and also before thee o king have I done no hurt'. King Darius has Daniel released and the men who had accused him were themselves cast into the den of lions,

along with their children, and their wives; and the lions had a mastery of them and brake all their bones in pieces' (verse 24). Furthermore, the king made a decree that in every dominion of his kingdom men tremble and fear before the God of Daniel for he is the living God with an everlasting dominion; for 'he worketh signs and wonders in heaven and earth delivering Daniel from the power of the lions'. Here we see that what the enemy meant for evil, God meant it for good and Daniel prospered in the reign of Darius and in the reign of Cyrus the Persian (verse 28).

f) When faith is coupled with praise

If we praise and thank God for the expected end, God will honour our faith in him because we align ourselves with His will and His Word. Jehoshaphat, King of Judah heard from the Lord and put faith into action. We recall history at the time when the Moabites and the Ammonites came against Jehoshaphat to battle in **2 Chronicles 20**. All Judah stood before the Lord and looked to him and the Spirit of the Lord came upon Jahaziel who told them that **'the battle is not yours, but God's'.** He also told them that the next day they were to meet them by the cliff of Ziz, at the end of the brook before the wilderness of Jeruel. In this battle they needed not to fight, but to stand still and see the salvation of the Lord with them (see verse 17). So all Judah and Jerusalem bowed down and worshipped the Lord God of Israel when they heard this message. They accepted it obediently, early in the morning, they all travelled to that part of the wilderness, chosen by God and were exhorted to 'Believe in the Lord your God, so shall ye be established, believe his prophets, so shall ye prosper' by, Jehoshaphat. Faithfully Jehoshaphat consulted the people and appointed singers unto the Lord who should praise the beauty of holiness as they went out before the army. The moment they began to sing and utter the words 'Praise the Lord for his mercy endureth for ever' the Lord took over and caused their enemies to destroy themselves utterly, 'none escaped' (see verse 24). What really happened in this story? The people had faith in God and trusted Him to fight for them. Did they question their leader who asked them to sing and praise God instead of using carnal weapons? On the 4th day, Jehoshaphat led them again into Jerusalem with joy, for the Lord had made them to rejoice over their enemies (see verse 27). 'They came to Jerusalem with psalteries and harps and trumpets unto the house of the Lord. And the fear of God was on all the kingdoms of those countries when they had heard that the Lord fought against the enemies of Israel'. Evidently, when faith is coupled with praise, victory is assured.

g) Lessons from the evidence

It is quite evident that victory comes through obedience in worship in the case of Joshua, Daniel and Jehoshaphat. That's where God's heart is located—True Worship. Sometimes when you are asked in church to raise your hands/stand up/shout the highest note of praise, some people disobey and because we were not all obedient we did not have the victory or the blessing. In **1 Samuel 15:22,** Samuel asked the question: Hath the Lord as great delight in burnt offerings and sacrifice, as in obeying the voice of the Lord? He was furious 'when the people took the spoil, sheep and oxen, the chief things which should have been utterly destroyed, to sacrifice unto God in Gilgal . . . and he spared Agag also'. In verse 22 Samuel continues to exhort us to obey God. He states: 'Behold to obey is better than to sacrifice and to hearken than the fat of rams'. So then, when we are in Church let us unite and receive blessings from the Lord, for it is better to obey than to offer any type of sacrifice to God. If you obey, you too will be able to give God thanks and God will be pleased with your sacrifice. King Saul was not able to give God thanks because he obeyed the voice of the people instead of God's. The prophet told Saul that because he had rejected the word of the Lord, the Lord had rejected him from being king over Israel (verse 27); and also repented that he had made Saul king over Israel (verse 35). What a lesson!

Conclusion

This study has made me realise that there is a greater joy associated with those who praise, worship and thank God for his loving kindness and tender mercies throughout the ages; and I trust you have too. Whether it is rendered personally or corporately, we have seen how those who use the spiritual weapon of praise never fail to cause God to demonstrate his power. In the examples sited in Scripture with Joshua, David, Jehoshaphat, Daniel and the Samaritan woman, we observed that God always manifests his power through the vehicle of Praise/Worship/ Thanksgiving. Therefore I cannot help but to agree with Dr David. L. Robbins (2008) when he states: 'Praise is the vehicle of faith that brings us into the presence and power of God' for there is no end to praising God; this is a lifestyle for the saints of God.

Bibliography

AMG'S Annotated Strong's Hebrew Dictionary of the Old Testament, AMG Publishers, 2003

Collins Double Book Enclyclopedia and Dictionary, Wm. Collins Sons & Co. Ltd., 1968

Kauflin, B. (2008) Worship Matters, Leading others to encounter the greatness of God

Noster, P. (1995) Creation at Worship: Ecology, Creative and Christian Worship

Reader's Digest Reverse Dictionary, The Reader's Digest Association Limited, 1989

Redemption Songs, 1000 Hymns and Choruses, HarperCollins Publishers, Hymn 459

The New Collins Thesaurus, Guild Publishing London, A Creative A-Z Word finder in Dictionary Form, 1984

Webber, Robert, E. (1996) Blended Worship: Achieving Substance and Relevance in Worship, Hendrickson Publishers

Yoshiaki, H. (1982) Worship: Adoration and Action, Theology of Worship in the Old Testament, Portland, p21

Zie'l, (2010) Every time I get a chance to praise him—**U-Tube**

Online Sources

http://www.En.wikipedia.org/Wiki, the free Encyclopedia/**Harvest Festivals**, 30 May 2012

http://www.praise-and-worship.com

http://www.higherpraise.com/worship/worship_worshipisalifestyle

http://www.gotquestions.org/Christian—worship.html/**What is the meaning of Christian Worship?**

http://www.Praise-and-worship.com/**Praise and worship the God of the Bible for he is holy and righteous**

About the Author

When a Christian believer's praise turns into worship, a great power is unleashed. Praise, Worship, and Thanksgiving seeks to inspire you to become a worshipper in order to understand that power. Author Audrey Eccleston shows how praise and worship were used as a weapon by the children of Israel in the Old Testament, under the leadership of Jehoshaphat, Daniel, and Joshua. She further explains that whenever praise and worship were used in this manner in Bible times, the awesome presence of God always brought sure victory to God's people.

Praise, Worship, and Thanksgiving illustrates the steps you can to take to become a worshipper. While fully describing what praise and worship are to Christians, Eccleston also offers guidance on why, how, and when to praise and worship God. She provides powerful truths from the Scripture for use by those who have faith in God and observations on the differences among praise and worship; the theory and practice of praise; and the theory and practice of worship and thanksgiving.

Praise, Worship, and Thanksgiving presents a vital manual on worshipping to provide a full-scale "how to" course in all of the essentials.

Printed in the United States
By Bookmasters